A Day in the Life: Rainforest Animals

Macaw

Anita Ganeri

www.raintreepublishers.co.uk
Visit our website to find out more information about Raintree books.

To order:
☎ Phone 0845 6044371
📄 Fax +44 (0) 1865 312263
✉ Email myorders@raintreepublishers.co.uk

Customers from outside the UK please telephone +44 1865 312262

Raintree is an imprint of Capstone Global Library Limited, a company incorporated in England and Wales having its registered office at 7 Pilgrim Street, London, EC4V 6LB – Registered company number: 6695582

Edited by Nancy Dickmann, Rebecca Rissman, and Catherine Veitch
Designed by Steve Mead
Picture research by Mica Brancic
Originated by Capstone Global Library
Printed and bound in China by South China Printing Company Ltd

ISBN 978 1 4062 1784 1 (hardback)
14 13 12 11 10
10 9 8 7 6 5 4 3 2 1

ISBN 978 1 4062 1878 7 (paperback)
15 14 13 12 11
10 9 8 7 6 5 4 3 2 1

British Library Cataloguing in Publication Data
Ganeri, Anita
Macaw. -- (A day in the life. Rainforest animals)
598.7'1-dc22
A full catalogue record for this book is available from the British Library.

Acknowledgements
We would like to thank the following for permission to reproduce photographs: Alamy **pp. 14, 23 flock** (© Wildlife GmbH); Ardea **p. 11** (Andrea Florence); Corbis **pp. 5** (© Ted Horowitz), **9** (Science Faction/© Stuart Westmorland), **18, 19, 20, 21, 23 roost** (© Frans Lanting); FLPA **pp. 7** (Minden Pictures/Tim Fitzharris), **12** (Minden Pictures/Pete Oxford), **13, 23 rubbery** (© Frans Lanting); Photolibrary **pp. 4** (Picture Press/Juergen & Christine Sohns), **6** (John Warburton-Lee Photography), **10** (Superstock/Joe Vogan), **15, 23 clay** (age fotostock/Morales Morales), **16** (Robin Smith), **17, 23 toucan** (Oxford Scientific (OSF)/Carol Farneti Foster), **22** (imagebroker.net/jspix jspix); Shutterstock **p. 23 rainforest** (© Szefei).

Cover photograph of a red macaw parrot reproduced with permission of Corbis (Brand X/© Steve Allen).

Back cover photographs of (left) a macaw's wing reproduced with permission of Photolibrary (Picture Press/Juergen & Christine Sohns); and (right) a macaw's claw reproduced with permission of FLPA (Minden Pictures/Tim Fitzharris).

We would like to thank Michael Bright for his invaluable help in the preparation of this book.

Every effort has been made to contact copyright holders of material reproduced in this book. Any omissions will be rectified in subsequent printings if notice is given to the publisher.

Contents

Some words are in bold, **like this**. You can find them in the glossary on page 23.

What is a macaw?

beak

wing

A macaw is a type of bird.

All birds have wings and beaks and their bodies are covered in feathers.

Macaws belong to a group of birds called parrots.

Macaws can be many different colours.

Macaws have brightly coloured feathers.

But it is not easy to see them among the leaves and fruit of the **rainforest** trees.

claw

Macaws have strong toes and sharp claws for gripping branches.

They have large, curved beaks for eating food.

Where do macaws live?

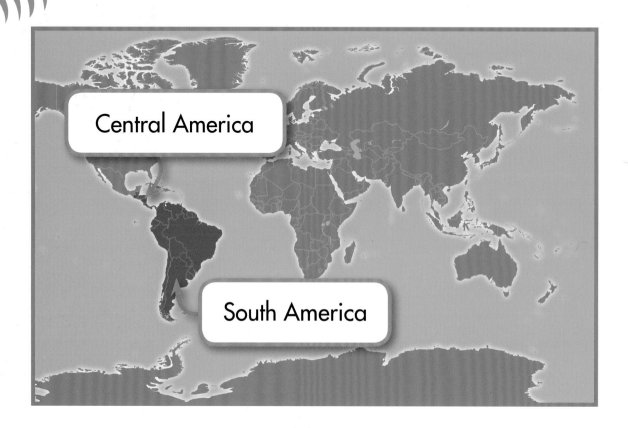

Central America

South America

Macaws live in the **rainforests** of Central America and South America.

It is warm and wet in the rainforest all the year round.

In the rainforest, macaws live among the trees and along the riverbanks.

Some types of macaws also live on mountains and grasslands.

What do macaws do in the day?

Macaws usually wake up just before the sun rises.

They clean their feathers with their beaks and call to tell each other where they are.

Then the macaws fly off to find some fruit trees and start feeding.

At midday, they rest in the shade and then feed again in the afternoon.

What do macaws eat?

Macaws mainly eat fruit, nuts, seeds, flowers, and leaves.

They also eat small animals, such as insects and snails.

tongue

A macaw holds a nut in its foot and crushes the shell with its strong beak.

It gets the nut out with its beak and **rubbery** tongue.

Do macaws live in groups?

Macaws live in large groups called **flocks**.

In the day, the flock flies off together to look for food.

clay

Sometimes, the flock flies to a cliff by the river and eats the **clay** soil.

The clay helps the macaws' bodies take in the food they need.

What do macaws sound like?

Macaws make loud screeching and squawking sounds.

The sounds help them to keep in touch with each other.

toucan

Macaws also call to warn each other of danger.

Enemies, such as **toucans**, like to eat the macaws' eggs and chicks.

Where are baby macaws born?

A female macaw lays her eggs in a nest inside a hollow tree.

She sits on the eggs until they hatch.

chick

When the chicks hatch, their parents look after them and bring them food.

Later, the chicks grow their flight feathers and learn to fly.

What do macaws do at night?

In the evening, the macaws fly to trees to **roost**.

They squabble and squawk as they work out where to sit.

The macaws fluff out their feathers to keep warm.

Then they sleep through the night.

Macaw body map

wing

feathers

eye

beak

foot

tail

Glossary

 **clay** type of soil

 **flock** large group of birds

 **rainforest** thick forest with very tall trees and a lot of rain

 **roost** sit on a branch and go to sleep

 **rubbery** soft and bendy

 **toucan** rainforest bird with a large, colourful beak

Find out more

Books

Rainforest Animals (Focus on Habitats), Stephen Savage (Wayland, 2006)

Usborne Beginners: Rainforest, Lucy Beckett-Bowman (Usborne, 2008)

Websites

http://animals.nationalgeographic.co.uk/animals/birds/macaw.html

www.belizezoo.org/zoo/zoo/birds/mac/mac1.html

Index